JHB: Inside Speaking Out

JHB: Inside Speaking Out

Words Apart

JHB

To order additional copies of this book, contact:
Xlibris Corporation
1-888-795-4274
www.Xlibris.com
Orders@Xlibris.com
100061

Contents

Dedication

I am grateful to have my family (Dad, Doug, Brandon, Luke, Keisha, Isaac, Gracie, Eric, Jennifer, Emily, Danielle) and I appreciate all my friends (Wills, Boo, Tim, Flakes, Jason, Lauren). But there are 3 people I want to give a special thank you. My Mom Theresa, who I simply owe everything to. She is to blame for every good quality I have. I have the best mom out there and I'm thankful for her everyday of my life. I want to mention my Sister Amanda as well. She has shown me what it means to sacrifice and taught me what resolve means to achieving goals. You can find her within a lot of my convictions and I am proud to say she is my big sister. Then there's Whitney, a sincere friend in both good times and through the worst. I still remember what I thought the first time I laid eyes on her. And after getting to know her, my initial thinking was confirmed. Genuine in her beauty and amazing in her ways. The type of girl you find once in a lifetime . . . Together these 3 lovely ladies are the strongest women I know, I owe much of my inspiration to them. I could not ask for a better mom, a stronger sister or a more understanding friend . . .

-JHB

Acknowledgments:

Patience.

T's Woo

You know it truly is amazing.
Amazing what words can mean to somebody.
Words can inspire or sweet talk your deepest desire.
Words can be ones motivate. They can ask other words to translate.
Words can warm you up on a cold Wisconsin day. Words can show you direction, point you in the right way. They can crawl into spaces when nothing else fits. Words can be a sweet victory or in defeat surrender, I quit. Words often ask "can we talk". Sometimes words go missing, lost in a lonesome walk. Words can bring peace instead of waging war. Words declare chivalry is not dead as a gentleman opens a door. Words can simply greet "Hello", "How do you do", "Pleasure's all mine.", "See you soon!", "goodbye". Words have all the answers, able to explain everything. Who, What, Where and Why. Words can promise never to break a promise. So isn't it ironic Words are how most promises break? Anyways, back to Words . . . Words can give and Words can take . . . Words can bring you back to another time. Or bring a smile to your face with just a thoughtful rhyme . . . Words are how I describe your beauty in a story. Poets? No, it's Words that deserve the glory . . . Words, Word . . .

~JHB

PS—Words can be continued. To be continued . . .

Two Hearts . . .

Two Hearts, one of a kind,
Always finding each other in time.
No matter how harsh the fight,
These two hearts always beat together at the end of the night . . .
Both Hearts have said "I Love You"
And will continue to say it after all they go through.
After these three words were spoken,
Both Hearts knew as long as they had each other, they could never
be broken . . .

~JHB

Lullaby, Beautiful . . .

Close your eyes and put a smile on your face . . .
Slip out of reality have your worries erase . . .
Let your dreams fill with joy and pleasure . . .
Happiness so unforgettable that the real world can't measure . . .
Fall in Love! . . . Travel the stars or fly! . . .
In your dream lives a fantasy where you never have to say Goodbye . . .
Now fade away to a place we can always meet . . .
Enjoying relaxing and being off your feet . . .
When you wake I want to hear the adventures you went through . . .
Good night Beautiful, sleep sweet sings my lullaby to you . . .

~JHB

*I was out watching the Packer vs. Eagle football game, opening day. The game was close and getting intense. When this was happening I was getting a phone call from a friend. Deciding to figure out what was up I called her back and she broke the sad news that my friend Sam had killed himself. They say the "Good Die Young" because of people like Sam. His mom had just recently passed away after her fight with breast cancer for I try to find comfort in thinking they are up there together looking down on all us . . .

Sam . . . 9/9 Problems . . .

. . . It's opening day, all tied up with a chance to win . . .

My phone comes alive and I think "calling me right now is a classified sin" . . .
I decide it can wait and let it ring and ring and ring . . .
Then I felt a text message . . . Vibe Vibe followed by a PING . . .
"Call me right away" is a message I was unable to ignore . . .
Picking up my phone I headed out the door . . .
I found a quiet spot between two cars and sat down . . .
Possibly missing the game winner turned my smile into a frown . . .
Waiting for an answer on the other end . . .
Wondering why I would be needed right now as a friend . . .
"Hey what's up? You needed me to call?" . . .
Whimpers, sobs and stuttering sentences said nothing and said it all . . .
"What the hell are you talking about? What do you mean he is dead?" . . .
Unable to understand what I just heard, not accepting what was just said . . .
"No you're wrong! What you're telling me can't be true!" . . .
"I'll call you back." Hanging up I sat in disbelief, preparing what to do . . .
I collected my emotions and wiped away my eyes . . .
I tried to blend in as I took my seat with the other guys . . .
Excitement was intense as the kick was made and the game was won . . .

But I had just found out a little boy lost his Father and a Mother was
joined in Heaven by her Son . . .
The cheers were loud . . .
Our fans were proud . . .
I was able to go unnoticed, be left alone and not catch a stare . . .
Then all it took was someone showing an ounce of care . . .
"What was the phone call about?" asked someone's wonder . . .
My eyes answered with tears and I responded with a blunder . . .
Unable to comprehend and unable to speak . . .
The emotion was taking over and leaving me weak . . .
I make it through and finally leave the bar . . .
I drive to my mom's with two friends in my car . . .
As I pull up and park in the driveway . . .
It all hits me . . . My friend was here yesterday but dead today . . .
My feelings, still being contained as I walk in, quite as a mouse . . .
I feel a sense of Love and security anytime I enter this house . . .
I join my family and in silence sit down at the kitchen table . . .
My Mom asked me "How are you?" and I was no longer able . . .
No longer able to hold it in as I sat there letting people watch me cry . . .
Without hesitation or question my mom put her arms around me
before asking why . . .
Allowing me to drown in my tears and let it all out . . .
Proving unconditional Love, not knowing what my breakdown was about . . .
Finally asking and reassuring "What's wrong? Whatever it is, it will be ok" . . .

. . .I understood why my friend left, in the moment, on that day . . .

~JHB

Loving Fast, and Living in the Past

WHY?! . . . Why am I even asking myself this question? Why? . . .

Why . . . Do I still want to get lost in your eyes? . . .
Why . . . Do I still listen to your whys? . . .
Why . . . Do I make myself say sorry? . . .
you justify your actions by a bullshit story? . . .
Why . . . Do I want you back in my arms? . . .
Why . . . Do I still want to protect you from harm? . . .
Why . . . Do I still miss the taste of your kiss? . . .
Why . . . Why in the hell are you someone I would ever miss? . . .

My mind was cloudy until I heard those words "Me and her are together" . . .
In an instant the sun shined through, a break in my weather . . .

Benefit of the doubt, I opted to trust . . .
Thinking your word was enough, your Love was a must . . .
Now I feel regret, embarrassed and dumb . . .
You get credit for my emotions now going numb . . .

After hearing that news I turned off my phone . . .
Wanting to exist only in my solitude and be alone . . .
Hours later I turned it back on to hear what you had to say . . .
All I listened to was your silence of shame for over a day . . .
. . . Then you blamed me . . .
No, that's bullshit! Sorry . . .
It was my fault you went behind my back? . . .
It was my try that was the lazy, the lack? . . .
Stop acting like my Love, my intentions were never true . . .
make excuses for what you put me through? . . .
I stood up, against all reason for you . . . Against my friends . . .
Never questioning . . . Wanting you by my side in the end . . .
Your satisfaction was the focus of my mind . . .
too bad you wanted a dime a dozen rather than one of a kind . . .
Maybe not the guy who has always been in your dream . . .
But I'm the guy who you Love because I'm always as I seem . . .

History doesn't repeat itself, it's up to you . . . Stay or go back to your past . . .
But is it really that easy to forget the Love you fell for so fast . . .

trying to steer a derailed train back on the track . . .
Against all instincts, I want you back . . .
driving through Life, a growing depression each mile . . .
You are my detour, my sightsee, my smile . . .

. . . How do you let that go? . . . Open ended question, let me know . . .

~JHB

Honesty in your Eyes

Now I hate waking up . . .

My eyes staring blankly, blurring everything I don't want to see . . .
Dead inside, walking through life like a zombie . . .
I became naive, simply thinking a laugh could warm my heart . . .
Daydreaming during the days, a perfect world, we would never fall apart . . .

I used to wake up and couldn't wait to fade away back in my bed . . .
then I met you, started living my favorite dream and three words were
said . . .
I was losing touch with reality, expecting life to play out like in my mind . . .
I felt you were the girl, the one from my dream I knew I'd always find . . .

But now I hate waking up.
Alone once again . . .

I should have known it was too good to be true? . . .
Instead I foolishly trusted the honesty in your eyes when you claimed
"I Love you too" . . .

-JHB

11:11 Make a Wish

I now realize I was waiting for you to be her . . . Loving you because of
made up scenarios, thoughts in my head . . .
Well you're not her and I wasn't me . . . Finally a clear mind, my soul
is no longer dead . . .
*You had someone to write your Love story but my pen ran out of ink,
sorry*
Now when it rains and you want to dance . . .
Remember you wasted your last and final chance . . .

You showed me such a beautiful smile at first, your eyes flirted with me . . .
Now you show me an ugly face, in your eyes nothing to see . . .

*You may have forgotten I was that guy. Happiness and respect is what
you expected, why?*
You loved me first, kind of made me proud . . .
I was waiting for the right time, which turns out was never, to say it
out loud . . .

Using you to cure my troubles and prevent me from being alone . . .
You were nothing more than a cover . . .

Should have treated you like you deserved, a nameless Lover . . .

You let the affection fade . . . Showing you I care never the issue . . .
Always there, forever forgiving, painfully aware . . . How would you
have felt if I kissed her before I came to kiss you? . . .

You had it all wrong, letting me slip right away . . .
Not the one you find everyday . . . I am the one you find one day . . .

Patience is a virtue, practice it when you can . . . Trust me, I tried . . .
We could have had a future but in the present you lied . . .

Its 11:11 Make*a*Wish look up at the stars . . .
I would have reached up and grab them all for you, each one ours . . .

Now I get up with no good morning . . .
Still I smile at the day . . .
Because life is beautiful and I appreciate our time together, now fu*k
you, I'm on my way . . .

~JHB

*This was written after finding out my girlfriend at the time was cheating,
again. I don't regret accepting faults like insecurity, immaturity, no substance
or unable to hold an adult conversation but knows better for next time. She
had a great guy any girl would be lucky to have. Your loss Miss Sammy . . .
Fool me once shame on you, fool me twice shame on me . . . But Fu*k you!
*Side Note: 2 Red Flags . . . 1) If A girl asks randomly "Am I pretty?" . . . 2) She
sexts you before you are even dating . . . Beware of Sexter!!!*

GRANDPA

Dedicated to Grandpa and Grandma T

Who would have thought the life he lived would be so great? . . .
Orphaned and alone at the age of only 8 . . .
He did so many things in Life . . .
He protected our freedoms and married a dedicated wife . . .
He raised 12 Daughters and Sons . . .
He had an impact on everyone . . .
He had 34 Grandkids who he all Loved . . .
With one special one watching down from up above . . .
He lived each one of his 86 years . . .
A life full of happiness along with tears . . .
We all have our own memories to hold onto . . .
Until Heaven needs us, our time due . . .
He proudly believed in God . . .
And knew he was always just doing his job . . .
He died peacefully and got his last wish . . .
He is someone we are truly going to miss . . .
He'll forever be watching over us now . . .
Good Job Urban Titulaer, take a bow . . .

~JHB

I have a huge family and have somehow been blessed in the sense we haven't had to go through to many deaths. When my Grandpa T passed away I wanted to somehow comfort my mom and the only way I knew how was through writing. I wrote this the night before the funeral and when my mom read it she shared it with others in the family and it ended up being read at the service by our Priest. First experience moving people with my words and will forever be one of my proudest memories.

*My little brother was in an accident in which he suffered 3rd degree burns on 37% of his body . . . I wrote this the day after it happened. I'm so glad that our family turned a negative into a positive and came together for one another. A lot of people aren't fortunate enough to have the strength of family during tough times. The last two lines in poem were written with certainty. I'm proud of my brother Brandon for his attitude through all this, his ability to be happy rather than take the easy way out and become a victim. Everything happens the way it's supposed to, why this happened? I'm not sure yet? But maybe he wouldn't have met his future wife Emily (a girl that puts up with his sense of humor is a catch) or became a father to a beautiful baby girl, Gracie. I'm proud of all my siblings for their own reasons, all amazing. I'm proud of Brandon for not only making it through this but for doing it in an inspiring way. I'm not the best at showing it at times but I'm grateful for the family I have. I Love you all and send good thoughts to you every day.

Our Fire Fighter

Dedicated to Brandon

A Loving brother and a caring son . . .
Just a 13 year old having fun . . .

Who would have thought such an evil accident . . .
Could happen to a boy who was Heaven sent? . . .

In a matter of seconds his life changed forever . . .
On a beautiful Sunday day with record setting weather . . .

The Mother who, without hesitation, saved his life . . .
Is now overflowing with pain, cut deep, deeper than the sharpest knife . . .

His Father was by his side as soon as he could be . . .
Brandon knew he was there, even though unable to see . . .

Our step dad sat there, wishing there was more he could do . . .
But nobody expected this, what to do? Nobody knew . . .

His little Brother, innocent like most kids his age tend to be . . .
Saw something no one, any age, needs to see . . .

His older sister sat in the waiting room, a tear rolling down her face . . .
His older brother thinking, time to put grudges aside and as a family
embrace . . .

Grandparents, Aunts, Uncles, Cousins, Neighbors and Friends . . .
Gifts, thoughts and prayers were all they could send . . .

I just hope everyone knows, Brandon's one tough guy . . .
And even after all this he'll set his sights as high as the sky . . .

~JHB

Reflecting in reflections . . . part 1

I remember the first time I let you know I Loved you . . .

My nerves were making it hard but looking into your eyes helped me get through . . .
Tucking you into bed on that warm Florida night . . .
I felt so lucky glancing back at you before turning off the light . . .
You accepted me for me, flaws issues and all . . .
You walked by my side, helping me to stand tall . . .
Steady as my rock the times I wanted to give up . . .
Whenever I was negative, your Love always filled my cup . . .
In my future is where I saw you, patiently waiting for me . . .
A man without you is a man I did not want to be . . .
But then somewhere between Loving you and growing up I lost sight . . .
Instead of admitting my obvious faults, I became stubborn leading to a fight . . .
I started to care too much about my feelings and not enough about yours . . .
. . . My mom taught me how to be a gentleman . . .
Now not stopping to hold open doors . . .
Becoming so unkind . . .
So unaware stupidly blind . . .

Ignorant to the reasons behind your reactions . . .
Never taking blame for my consequential actions . . .
Neither of us were perfect but I'm mainly to blame . . .
I let not only you, but myself down, defining shame . . .
I saw it becoming bad but made no effort to fix it . . .
Thinking things would be better, maybe easier if I just quit . . .
Nothing can ever justify what I did . . .
If heartless came up at auction, I'd have the highest bid . . .

Nearly 4 years after smiling at the thought of you being the one . . .
We were done . . .

A reflective pause before closing our door behind me for the last
time . . .
Stepping into reality, realizing I just walked out on the rhythm that
inspired my rhyme . . .
Starting over brought on many emotions from excitement to feelings of
fear . . .
Sometimes I'd lay awake wondering were we sharing the same tear . . .
Countless nights of solitude fights within my mind . . .
Helped me figure out what it was I still needed to find . . .
And after overcoming my self-inflicted heartbreaking defeat . . .
I finally stood up, bruised and beat up but back on my feet . . .

I took advantage of the freedom and made some friendships stronger . . .
With nobody to answer to I allowed my fun nights to last longer . . .
The best part was being able to take the person I was when we met and
introduce him to the person I am now . . .
After meeting, they both asked each other the same question . . . "How?" . . .
"How did you get her?" . . . "How did you let a girl like her go?" . . .
Silent, with no answer, deciding to learn from the other and grow . . .
In time I once again felt like a good man . . .
Questioning if I could remain that way and thinking "Yes I can." . . .
Selfishly I gave another girl my heart . . .
Finding out the hard way Love doesn't conquer all and without attention
can fall apart . . .

I've learned what kind of person I have been, can be, and want to be
since you've been away . . .
Lately having the same thoughts, almost every day . . .
Wondering where would we have been if we worked it out? . . .
If we would have just Loved with no questions, without doubt? . . .

~JHB

Rough Draft of Romance . . .

I was at a point where my life was on a good path . . .
Before meeting her it was long division . . . After her it became simple math . . .
Together we learned life's side of maturity . . .
Forgetting though to deal with life's uncertainty . . .
We allowed ourselves to no longer appreciate each other anymore . . .
Myself more than her, we forgot how to compromise, slamming shut every door . . .
We went from the high of Loving each other to crashed, broken on the floor . . .

. . .Then I met her . . .
What I wanted to work on, wanted to fix became unsure . . .
Something about her drew me in . . .
My actions after that were shameful, a selfish sin . . .
Shrinking inside while I pretended to stand tall . . .
No longer able to live a lie I confessed, told all . . .
Looking back I didn't realizing what I was losing . . .
The pain couldn't be seen but inside it was bruising . . .
But at the time it was easy letting you go . . .
Thinking my feelings were certain for her, head to toe . . .
And I went for her, thinking she's what I needed all along . . .
At a time of extreme weakness she made me feel strong . . .
. . . Well eventually I got burned . . .
. . .Anyone in my shoes would have learned . . .
. . .Anyone not named me . . .

I still thought wrongly it could be . . .
Instead I was left. Just like that alone . . .
A lost King with a broken Throne . . .
  . . . Then came the girl certain to save my day . . .
  . . . The girl who took time to understand all my ways . . .
She was right in front of my eyes . . .
Never should have been a surprise . . .
A friend before anything more . . .
Someone who got me to my core . . .
Circumstances stopped me from pursuing in the past . . .
But I finally let it be & let fate decide if it'd last . . .
Going against even the wisest of advice . . .
Deciding feelings would be enough to survive, at least suffice . . .
I went for it, Love is just what I do . . .
My feelings undeniable, emotions true . . .
Knowing when she left it'd be hard . . .
Start of a romance was trumped by the college experience card . . .
Out of sight, out of mind . . .
Losing again what was so hard to find . . .
Go your path and find your way . . .
Remember me tomorrow but forget me today . . .

~JHB

Blame Game of Mistake . . .

Sometimes Love grows all it can grow . . .
It reaches an end and inside you just know . . .

You reflect on the mistakes you've made . . .
And can be overcome by the price that's been paid . . .

Suddenly your emotions are seduced by sadness . . .
Your mind instantly consumed by madness . . .

New chapters are always hardest to write . . .
Internal struggle being the hardest fight . . .

Love is the hardest feeling to find also the hardest to lack . . .
Making it easy to close your eyes and go back . . .

But is reliving memories what you really want to do? . . .
Think, were you able to be happy? Simply being you? . . .

Did you ever think it'd be so hard to enjoy in life? . . .
Wondering how you can find a smile in a big pile of strife? . . .

Once you get over the initial heartache . . .
And once and for all . . .
Stop playing the blame game of mistake . . .

Your heart will eventually mend . . .
For you see, joy cannot break, it can only bend . . .

Remind yourself "There is someone perfect out there for me . . ." . . .
Have faith close your eyes and you will eventually see . . .
P.S . . .
I might have left but I'm not going anywhere . . .
Good times and bad, sad faces or smiles, I'll always care . . .

~JHB

The Last Past . . .

I fumble through my key chain looking for my past . . .
Shaking as I open the door to my future which didn't last . . .
My footsteps hit the ground . . .
Silence, an unfamiliar sound . . .

My body gets tense anxiety starts to grow . . .
Used to walking in, greeted with a kiss hello . . .
I close my eyes and smell a home cooked meal . . .
Walking to the couch, ignoring telling you how I feel . . .

I open my eyes in confusion shaking my head . . .
"Thanks Beautiful, I Love you" is what I should have said . . .
I phase back to reality and start flipping on lights . . .
One by one I fade back to memories and start reliving our fights . . .

You screaming as loud as you can . . .
Me breaking character and taking it out on the fan . . .

Together we never learned how to solve a problem . . .
Our recipe of non-compromise and yelling did nothing to help them . . .

In our relationship I let the bad outweigh the good . . .
Hiding from the world by dropping my eyes and flipping up my hood . . .
I walk through darkness and stop at the kitchen sink . . .
You left dishes, knowing its my favorite time to think . . .

Putting away the clean, remembering where it all goes . . .
Sorting the silverware I sadly realize no one else knows . . .
Fork, Spoon, Spoon, Knife, Fork, Knife . . .
No one else knows or understands my life . . .

Who was there when my motivation started to wander, sometimes
slack? . . .
Your voice was clear as others mumbled behind my back . . .
Always there to support or break my downfall . . .
It was you who helped me through it all . . .

Overcome with sadness I flip off the lights and slowly shut the
door . . .
Wishing I could just collapse, letting my body hit the floor . . .
And as another silent tear falls off my face to the ground, to heavy to be
caught . . .
I know now, learning to fall out of Love while still appreciating that
person in your life, can be learned but it can not be taught . . .

~JHB

Sacrifice to Suffice

As life moves forward . . .
Ever wonder what it's toward? . . .
Each time you change your age . . .
Does it seem like you and life are on the same page? . . .
Each year you get older . . .
Do you feel yourself getting a little bit bolder? . . .
Are you more proud of what you do? . . .
Or still thinking not a millionaire by 25 your life is through? . . .
Maybe there's more confidence in your walk? . . .
Finding people to listening when you talk? . . .
Do friends see the new you, just found? . . .
Done walking on eggshells, scared to make a sound? . . .
Find that special someone who has you dreaming of I Do? . . .
It's nice, somebody there walking by your side, everything you go through . . .

I hope some of these are fact, if not . . ..

You'll stop comparing your life to your age, stop crying in your beers . . .
Eventually you'll stop keeping track of meaningless numbers in meaningful years . . .
You will understand your family comes first . . .
And Love contained is Love burst . . .
You'll still help those who ask, but never give more than you can? . . .
Finally realizing that some people take advantage of a hero over respecting a man . . .

THEN YOU'LL SEE . . .

Whether it is sports, TV, politics or fashion . . .
You'll get more passionate about your passion . . .
You'll care as much about you . . .
As you think everyone else should too . . .
All the experience of heartache, reliable pain . . .
Will have Prepared you for the harsh reality of life, a nicer word for INSANE . . .

IF YOU DON'T BELIEVE ME GO BACK FROM TODAYS DATE TO THE DAY . . .

Since the world first saw your eyes . . .
Has your journey been perfectly executed or has it been surprise after surprise? . . .

If you learn how to roll with the punches, have compassion and understand compromise . . .
You'll see that age is just a number defined by lies . . .

~JHB

Imag Dream

Imagine walking outside and the grass was blue and the sky was green . . .
All the rulers were gone, no more Presidents, Kings and God save the
Queen . . .

Everybody around you has lost their ability to frown . . .
The World you've known is turned upside down . . .

No more war or a need for fighting . . .
Rather than a consistent view, hate is a distant sighting . . .

Sharing the Love we all had at the moment of birth . . .
Finally! We did it! We have achieved Peace on Earth . . .

Now wake up from your dream and open your eyes . . .
Look out your window up into the skies . . .

You'll see what you always knew . . .
The grass is green and the sky always blue . . .

People will forever argue, disagree and debate . . .
We will Love to the end, but we will never forget how to Hate . . .

Our feelings all the same, just expressed in our own different way . . .
We all have thoughts and emotions that change from day to day . . .

The World could not be happy without knowing heartache . . .
Life gives us lessons we should always take . . .

Love the only feeling we're each born with, this fact is true . . .
But in order to grow up pain, anger and fear are all things we must go
through . . .

So all you can do is stare out your window and let life shine upon your
face . . .
Do not let the world's sadness make your day or life a waste . . .

Do not forget happiness starts from within . . .
And remember, smiling in the face of adversity is never viewed as a
sin . . .

But if you're having a hard time enjoying Life as it is, seeking
something to turn to . . .
Just close your eyes and imagine with me that the sky is green and the
grass is blue . . .

~JHB

Running out of Forever . . .

I feel you close, you whisper sweetly in my ear . . .
I close my eyes getting lost in what I hear . . .
Beautiful pictures of us run through my mind . . .
I never want to see again if Love is blind . . .
Everything's perfect in this simple moment of pleasure . . .
X might mark the spot but I already found my treasure . . .

My glass has sometimes been 1/2 empty . . .
Before you the bright side wasn't always easy to see . . .
Lady, if I were luck you'd be my 4-leaf clover . . .
And if I could stop time this moment would never be over . . .

You whisper softly . . .

"Your kiss is what I could never find but would always seek" . . .
Instantly overcome with joy a silent tear strolls down my cheek . . .

You deserve to hear how I feel . . .

That happiness is no longer an illusion now something real . . .
I want to tell you I'm sure in us when my fingers trace yours . . .
I want you to know you have the keys to my heart I want you to open every door . . .

My eyes closed I feel your breath on my skin . . .
   Time to express my emotions and let you in . . .
      I open my mouth to finally speak
         Thoughts are scrambled I feel weak . . .

Words can't escape, unable to say . . .

NO! Not now! Don't go silent . . . Today was the day! . . .

         My mind goes black and I hear no sound . . .
       My legs give in and I fall to the ground . . .
     I open my eyes and see you're not there . . .
Once in my life, vanished into thin air . . .

What was once a dream is now a nightmare haunting the thoughts inside my head . . .
If only I realized I didn't have forever to say the things I wanted said . . .

~JHB

To Fear? . . . Or Not to Fear? . . .

Some people fear facing reality . . .
Some fear losing gravity . . .
Some people fear falling in Love . . .
Some fear judgment from up above . . .
Some people fear Hate . . .
Some fear accepting fate . . .
Some people fear letting others down . . .
Some fear smiling, so they only frown . . .
Some people fear being alone in life . . .
Some fear friends walking behind them with a knife . . .
Some people fear failing . . .
Some fear never catching up, forever trailing . . .
Personally, my biggest fear in life are heights . . .
Others sleep with a night light, fearful of the unknown on moonless nights . . .
Some fears are physical, others in the head . . .
Hard to overcome internally fed . . .
Flying, Bungee jumping, skydiving are all fears that can be conquered within your brain . . . Acceptance, Appearance, Loneliness and Love are some fears that can drive you insane . . .
Sometimes I ramble and I tend to go off on a rant . . .
When I need to vent I pick up a pen . . . At times self-doubt tells me I can't . . .

Fearing people won't care about or understand what I have to share and say . . .
This is one of the many battles we face within ourselves every day . . .

. . . But no matter what I fear, don't patronize the struggles my mind goes through . . .

. . . Be it big or small, my fears affect me, and eventually could affect you all too . . .

Sometimes facing fear is like trying to slam a revolving door . . .

I try to remind myself it took fear for one man to lead an Army, to win a War . . .

"Fear is the beginning of wisdom." said WT Sherman . . .

Anything can be learned from fear . . . Even motivation, staying determined . . .

"The only thing we have to fear is fear itself." claimed our 32nd President . . .

The problem with that is not every solution to overcoming fear is evident . . .

Sadly, a lot of people I've met have more to fear beyond fear itself . . .

Unable to tap untapped emotional wealth . . .

Some fears are overwhelming . . . Such as "How can I keep the roof over our heads while still putting food on the table?" Or "How can I teach my kids anything is possible when I'm not even able" . . . Sometimes your hands slip off the wheel and you lose the ability to steer . . .

Things like guilt or shame make things more complicated than just dealing with that fear . . .

Then there are fears such as "I have to speak in front of class?" . . .

"But I'm afraid! What happens if I look like an ass?" . . .

These are the fears that you, along with the help from yourself, can make it through . . .

Anyone who is someone knows exactly how it feels to face self-doubt yet still do what they needed to do . . .

I wonder, is it actually possible, or even healthy for one to overcome all fear? . . .
Can doubt in one self be good for the mind? Somehow helping it become clear? . . .
The mind is a powerful tool. Memories, Dreams and Knowledge are just a few things it can create . . .
While facing fear your mind is completely consumed, it forces you to focus, to think, sparking an internal debate . . .
While standing there, stuck within your thoughts, pausing life to hesitate . . .
Remember that just knowing your fear is accepting your fate . . .
We face fear everyday . . .
Each of us in a different way . . .
It seems to me though, that fear is being taught but not everyone is learning . . .
People seeing fear but ignoring the good and becoming ignorant to the wisdom is concerning . . .
Do we teach Love and learn from Hate? . . .
Or are the only emotions we grow from the ones that make us feel great? . . .
Do we study every tear and memorize each smile? . . .
If we don't appreciate every feeling then feelings will never be worthwhile . . .
So Unless we grow day by day and become more aware year after year . . .
Self-doubt will spread to every corner of your mind and fear will breed fear . . .

~JHB

* I wrote this the night before I went to visit my girlfriend at the time who had just went away to college. I gave it to her as I left. It was a great feeling to write how I thought we'd feel seeing each other and an even greater feeling those things.

You are Sunshine

As I drive away . . .
There are some things I want to say . . .
This road ahead of me is long . . .
These feelings of missing you already strong . . .
Seeing you smile brought goose bumps to my skin . . .
Kissing your lips brought smiles from within . . .
Holding your hand made me want to think out loud . . .
I Love you're in my life. You make me so proud . . .
So let's talk about why you give me these feelings of joy . . .
What makes me want you to be my girl and me be your boy? . . .
I Love the happiness you bring to everything you do . . .
I Love the faith and conviction and the fact you hold it true . . .
I Love you wisdom beyond your years . . .
I Love the empathy we share that sometimes brings tears . . .
I Love you have such a generous heart . . .
I Love you haven't let distance keep us apart . . .
I Love you that you get my sense of humor . . .
I Love that "you and me" is a true rumor . . .
I'm well on my back to Green Bay . . .
But there are still a few more things I would like to say . . .
A long time ago you were there in front of my face . . .
I was busy sprinting through life when I needed to pace . . .
At times I have doubts and fears . . .
That along with bringing you happiness, I might bring you tears . . .
I promise to try and be the man of your dreams . . .
No matter what it takes or how hard it seems . . .

You're going to be successful no matter what you do . . .
Yet I'm still proving myself, out of struggles I've been through . . .
I've made mistakes in my past . . .
Hopefully this gray cloud above me doesn't last . . .
The difference between bad guys and me . . .
Is mistakes opened my eyes and allowed me to see . . .
I'm a good guy and my heart is true . . .
Let go of reservations & let me prove it to you . . .
I want you in my life . . .
Sharing happiness, joy, pain sometimes strife . . .
I will treat you like the Princess you are . . .
I want to fall in Love . . . Like this drive Have this relationship go far . . .

~JHB

Three Words . . .

What's the one thing you would say? . . .
Speaking to your loved one on your last day? . . .
Three simple words would say so many things . . .
Before you hear the bells of angels ring . . .

The three words don't have to be "I Love You" . . .
But rather . . . "I Thank You" . . .

I Thank You for being with me through the good times and bad . . .
I Thank You for comforting me when my face only communicated sad . . .
I Thank You for holding me in your arms so secure, so tight . . .
I Thank You for being by my helpless side day and night . . .
I Thank You for reliving me of my strife . . .
I Thank You for being THE ONE in my life . . .
I Thank You for being beautiful in all the possible ways . . .
I Thank You for Loving me during these last few days . . .
I Thank You for Loving me after all we've been through . . .
I Thank You for letting me be me and allowing me Love you . . .

I Thank You . . .

I Love You . . .

~JHB

Footstep Roller Coaster

Silent tears fall the heaviest off your face . . .
Symbols of the memories you can't erase . . .
Your cries, yells & screams are never found . . .
A sense of peace overcoming, quieting your sound . . .
Realizing your lifestyle isn't for the test of time . . .
Understanding its full of rhythm that doesn't always rhyme . . .
Like mountains building a snowball . . .
Life stands you up, so you can again fall . . .
But focus on the after & not the before . . .
Think about being on top, still dreaming on the 1st floor . . .
Reading "Life for Dummies", fighting happiness with
every page you turn . . .
Lessons becoming something you look forward to, appreciate &
always willing to learn . . .
Staring back at your past, on your face, a smile . . .
Remember each footstep you stepped, in every mile . . .

~JHB

Words for you Smile

I've been in Love before but never like this . . .
From the way you speak through your eyes to your . . .
Your Love expressed through a kiss . . .
The only way I think to explain it is simple, "True Love" . . .
At times making as much sense as cold weather, 2 hands 1 glove . . .
Listen, I know I get stuck in my ways . . .
Stubborn and uncompromising, sometimes for days . . .
I know that's not how you deserve to be treated . . .
I have to inhale my pride, not let my Love be conceited . . .
Remember the first night we hung out, you stole a kiss from my cheek? . . .
Your affection combined with words made me weak . . .
Didn't care about anything besides getting to know this girl, this person . . .
Yes, at times your name was one I was cursing . . .
. . . But through it all I've always Loved you . . .
. . . Feeling safe saying that knowing you Love me too . . .
You are wonderful. You have an amazing heart . . .
A daughter your parents can be proud of, as Beautiful as you are Smart . . .
. . . In no time you've become my favorite book . . .
"Once upon a while, they could just tell" . . .
Well? Have I earned your trust? Shown you the "whys"?
Why? Why it's not to good to be true, I'm different than other guys . . .
. . . .
Now I miss being that guy you used or used to Loved. And I miss you . . .
Can we go back in time? Change what happened? Pretend cheating isn't something you do? . . .
Thanks life for never teaching your lessons the easy way . . .
Why can't we live each yesterday like it were today? . . .

~JHB

Me Once, Not Me Twice

Always the right guy, the wrong time . . .
Always the rhythm never the rhyme . . .
I know I Love, I know how I feel . . .
Always expressed when it isn't allowed to be real . . .
Will you and I ever be "we" . . .
Or am I wasting my time wanting more than just me? . . .
My heart beats but it can also break . . .
Staring into your smile wondering if it's a risk I'm willing to take . . .
You fill me up with endless joy . . .
Though sometimes I just feel like your emotional play toy . . .
Can you answer are you worth playing the waiting game? . . .
Will your feelings for me ever be constant? Will you ever feel the
same? . . . .
I can tell how you feel when I'm with you . . .
I see the pain away of what you've been and are going through . . . .
When I hold you and our bodies come together tight . . .
I know I'm not the only one who feels this is right . . .

You know you deserve better than every other guy . . .
I'm the sliver of sun in your cloudy sky . . .
So put on your sunglasses, open your eyes wide . . .
See with me you will always have someone no matter what by your
side . . .
You let me slip away once before . . .
Looking into your eyes made me reopen the door . . .

Bad choices are something everyone makes . . .
We've since learned from my mistakes . . .
In the past I was insecure . . .
Overcome with skepticism delusional with fear . . .
You fell in Love with me without even trying . . .
I felt like that emotion was dying . . .
Closing that chapter in my book . . .
Never thinking you'd come back, an Angel face with the Devil's hook . . .

I'm a happy person, an amazing soul . . .
Now seeing your smile is one of my goals . . .
Consider this our second chance . . .
Let go, follow my lead and just dance . . .
Get over the moments of artificial joy which only last until the next
day . . .
Grab my hand, kiss my lips and, let's make our memories, what do
you say? . . .

Before you answer I want you to know you're amazing, the most
beautiful sight I've seen . . .
And no matter what, even if I'm a lonesome King, you'll always, in my
eyes, be a Queen . . .

~JHB

Women . . . What I Love . . . What I Hate . . .

Hi . . . My name is Josh and I Love women. I respect them and I appreciate the things they can do that nobody else can. My mom and sister would kill me if I were so ignorant. But women, similar to kids, can really bother you. It got me wondering, what are the things I Love about women and what are some things that I Hate about women . . . Rather than ignore the thought, hoping it went away, I took out my pen and started listing what came to mind.

Let's start on a positive note. First I should let you know when I say "they" I am referring to females. The Z snap "what do you mean by they?! . . ." is not needed. It just makes it easier. One thing I Love is "they" understand sides of you a lot of people don't. That allows you to become more comfortable and confident with whom you are. They also have a tendency to think its ok to be hypocritical in the relationship. It is fine with me if my girlfriend expects me to let her know what I'm doing; try not to ignore her all night, don't flirt, don't text girls behind her back, basic expectations. Yet it is always ok when they do those same things that they would get mad at. I Hate that. That reminds me of a classic woman move, instead of just telling us why they are mad they say "it's fine, I won't be mad" . . . Then get mad! Why are they are still allowed to get away with that?! Then again, something as simple as their laugh can make you smile, which I Love.

One thing that seems to be common female trait is they assume you want every girl you talk to. Jealously is a human emotion, so it's understandable. But when they start doing this next thing I Hate, understanding is out the window. Sometimes they argue with you for no real reason and don't even try to hide the fact they're basing their assumptions on nothing! I Hate that! I do Love though that they are always by your side and will be the one there in the end. And I Love that on that journey to the end they, in the hard times, can make you feel like everything is going to be alright.

Some guys would Hate this next one but I happen to Love it. I Love when they team up with my mom or sister. Even if they are devising a plan to prank me or embarrass me, I'm still happy. Who wouldn't be? Seeing the women you Love and care about get along. Thinking back to when I talked about how they can make everything seem alright. I should also add that along with being able to make you the happiest, they can also make you feel the worst. Sometimes they do this in spite but are always honest and sometimes they only do it because they worry, which I Love.

Through trial and error I've gained some knowledge and I Hate when they think we don't realize they are playing a game. Depending on the game, I find myself Loving it. And if not, Hating it. Something about being kept on my toes. I Love when they appreciate it if you do a romantic thing. It gives us nice, thoughtful guy's time to shine. On that same subject I Hate when they expect a guy to do romantic things even when he isn't a gentleman on a daily basis. If he wasn't taught how to even be a gentleman, he wasn't taught how to be sweet . . .

The list, even though short, tells me something. I noticed that the things I Hate about women, if not trivial, are just part of growing up. Would I put up with those things all my life? Not a chance. Could I tolerate them as growing pains if eventually they got better? Without question.

I think when you are young you might have unrealistic expectations. It would be nice if everything went as you imagined. Are you going to throw every relationship away at the first sign of reality? Spend your life forever looking for a fantasy? It might, and I hope it does work for you. I learned from my dad though that a man doesn't run away from his problems, he works through them. People who make it through tough situations usually come out of it stronger. Why would this logic change when people enter a relationship? It's ok to talk, argue, bicker, annoy and disagree. In life, I can promise hard times will come, I only hope you have a strong woman by your side when they do.

Earlier I said women are similar to kids. I now realize how similar. You Love your kids unconditionally. You may get mad at them, or they may do something you can't conceive but throughout it all you stand by their side, unashamed of that Love. Confident that they will learn from experience and become the person you know they can be because of it. I've been in Love before, each different. First Love, Live-in Love, Lustful Love, Best friend Love, Maybe more than friends Love and True Love . . .

If any of said Loves had hurt me, cheated, changed or did anything that is understandably not forgivable, I would have not been able to show patience like with the things I just mentioned . . . There is such a thing as unforgivable in unconditional.

The way I act on my way to maturity might have a big affect also on how they act. I know ladies have plenty of things they hate about us. As you get older you need to wiser and those reasons will fade.

Everything I Hate about women is all part of everything I Love in women. Everything I Love about women is things that will forever be.

You can't put a price on saying "I Love you" with only a glance. The moment, you know the one, when you look at the person you Love and a sense of calm, of pure joy overtakes you . . . That moment makes it all worth it.

I'm not delusional in my thinking. Love isn't all rainbows and unicorns. I understand the naive joy that it brings some people but when I Love someone they will see me cry, hear me yell, listen to me complain and if they are able to do that then they will see me succeed, hear me laugh and listen to their heart when it's happy. What else would the point be in saying "In good times and bad . . . ? For Richer or for Poorer . . . In Sickness and in Health . . . ."? When I say "I do" I will.

What do I Love about women? This . . . What do I hate about women? That . . .

~JHB

A Goodnight Kiss . . .
A Wait, One More . . .

I want a girl who knows her worth. All while making my world smile.
I want a girl who knows how to begin again. Who knows life isn't
something you simply win.
A girl who sees within the sin. I want a girl with genuine expectations.
Did I mention my intentions are in your best interest? You interested?
I want a girl who can turn to me. Count on my eyes when she needs me to see.
I want a girl who is sincere in 20 years when I hear I Love you.
Up, Down, Good, Bad and all I go through.
I want a girl who actually keeps her promise to stay true.
True synonyms; real, genuine, faithful, right and actual.
When I write it, the Love story's not fiction and the feelings are factual.
I want a girl who isn't just good enough for me but is good enough for
herself. I want a girl who turns me on. Often enough is enough.
I want a girl who can brighten my day. Too day turns night and
I want a girl who can keep that night bright. Lighting up every room
She walks into. Out of nowhere sneaking a hello kiss. A girl who
understands I can't
Grant her every wish. I want a girl who appreciates the little things. The
some hows, the somewhere, the some things. Who knows with me she
can accomplish anything. The answer to my who, what, where, when
and why. Someone who can convince me that even with a broken wing
you can still fly. A girl who is in it if she's in it. Who knows assured Love
insures Love. Insured Love is the Love I give to my Love.
I want a girl who sees what I see. That her beauty doesn't get better with
age but minute by minute. Step by Step, a girl who stands by my side
grabs my hand and enjoys the ride.
I want a girl who is not just my girlfriend but a best friend.
I want a girl who will someday be my happily ever after, the end.

~JHB

Nobody knows what I was thinking when my head hit the ground . . .
Nobody knows the silence I heard, a deafening sound . . .
Nobody felt the calm that overcame at my Aunts voice . . .
Nobody felt the shame, thinking this was my fault, a result of my choice . . .
Nobody knows why Katie is the only one I wanted Jocelyn to call . . .
Nobody knows why I only allowed my family to catch me in my fall . . .
Nobody remembers how safe I felt cuddling with Sammy in my hospital bed . . .
Nobody remembers how everything was ok with her whisper, "I Love you" said . . .
Nobody appreciates my mom and all selfless things she did . . .
Nobody appreciates my solitude, the places I went, places I hid . . .
Nobody understands how the thought of Whitney help me . . .
Nobody understands how in my darkness I still smiled, I could still see . . .
Nobody thought a lifelong friendship would end . . .
Nobody thought my heart would actually break not just bend . . .
Nobody can realize what was on my mind, this life changing bad memory stained time . . .
But nobody should expect I won't try to paint you a picture. Sticks and stones broke my bones, but my words will forever rhyme . . .

~JHB

"Envy is not an emotion my Empathy allows me to have."

"Tell me something that will make me smile and I'll promise it will make you smile."

"The best advice to follow is the one that wasn't . . ."

"But no matter, don't patronize the struggles my mind goes through . . . Whether big or small, my struggles affect me, and eventually could affect you too."

"We teach Love and learn from Hate."

"Remember me tomorrow but forget me today . . ."

"I still fall asleep tomorrow hoping I'll wake up next to you today . . ."

"Poetry is life's version of a Fairy Tale . . ."

"True Love is found in patience; Your soulmate is found through virtue."

"Since the world first saw your eyes, has your journey been planned out, perfectly executed or rather surprise after surprise?"

"Do you still help those who ask, but never give more than you can? Have you realized that some people take advantage of a hero rather than respecting a man . . ."

"Learn to fall out of Love but still appreciate that time in your life. It can be learned but cannot be taught . . ."

"People will forever argue, disagree and debate. We will Love to the end and will never not Hate."

"Love is the only feeling we are born with, fact is true . . . But in order to grow up; pain, fear and hurt are things we need to go through."

"Eventually it has to be realized the song you're playing for everyone else is not perfect. But heard by plenty, intriguing too many and if you're lucky, beautiful to a few."

"Life is overweight and fact is fat . . ."

"Expression is my form of flattery . . ."